Railways & Recollections
1969

Contents

© Chris Harris, 2012

Photos: © The NOSTALGIA Collection archive unless otherwise credited.

First published in 2012

British Library Cataloguing in Publication Data
A catalogue record for this book is available from the British Library.

ISBN 978 1 85794 398 6

Silver Link Publishing Ltd
The Trundle
Ringstead Road
Great Addington
Kettering
Northants NN14 4BW

Tel/Fax: 01536 330588
email: sales@nostalgiacollection.com
Website: www.nostalgiacollection.com

Printed and bound in Ceská Republika

Frontispiece: **BUCKFASTLEIGH** This delightful rural Great Western scene, with a pannier tank sandwiched in the middle of a four-coach auto-train, was recreated in April 1969 on the newly reopened Dart Valley Railway. Horses in the field are unconcerned as the locomotive powers its train from Buckfastleigh towards Staverton Bridge. *Brian Jackson*

Introduction: Man reaches the Moon

'One small step for man, one giant leap for mankind.' So spoke Neil Armstrong as he became the first human being to set foot on the Moon at 0256 GMT on Monday 21 July 1969. This history-making event, broadcast by television stations around the world, has to be the defining moment of the year. What had been the stuff of science-fiction for so many years was now a reality, and we all shared in the excitement of the success of the Apollo 11 mission.

Quite distinct from journeys into space, there were also several 'firsts' for ordinary air travel in 1969: Concorde made its first test flight, the Boeing 747 'Jumbo' jet also made its debut, and the Hunter jump jet entered service with the RAF. On the seas, the liner RMS *Queen Elizabeth 2* set sail on the North Atlantic between Southampton and New York.

The situation on the railways in Britain was one of ongoing change. Steam had finally disappeared entirely from the British Rail network in August of the previous year, and the new corporate identity was beginning to make inroads across the system, eliminating the regional colour schemes and, in the case of some stations, pre-nationalisation signage. In 1969 the process was far from complete, and there were still plenty of stations that had not been touched by modernisation. Moreover, pre-war electric stock was still in regular use in some areas, making it possible to enjoy a timeless nostalgic experience, if you knew where to look. I can remember realising that these delights would not be around for very much longer, and recall making a number of journeys simply to enjoy the atmosphere while it lasted.

Sadly, there were some very significant closures in 1969. The year began particularly badly, with the withdrawal of services over the Waverley Route between Carlisle and Edinburgh from 6 January; the same date also saw the cessation of passenger trains between Leuchars Junction and St Andrews in Scotland. The line from Darlington to Richmond in North Yorkshire succumbed in March, while May closures included the former Great Central route between Rugby and Nottingham, the line between Stratford-upon-Avon and Honeybourne, and also Manchester Central and Manchester Exchange stations. Preservationists now run steam trains over part of the old Great Central line between Leicester and Loughborough, while the erstwhile Manchester Central is now an exhibition and conference centre. The official date for closure between Lewes and Uckfield was also May 1969, but in this case the condition of a viaduct had given rise to concern, and buses had replaced trains on this section of route since 24 February, although until May you had to buy a ticket from a station in order to travel on the replacement bus. Chandler's Ford station, between Eastleigh and Romsey, was closed to passengers in May

1969, although the line remained in use and the station was reopened in 2003. October saw the closure of Chester Northgate station and also the line between Dereham and Wymondham in East Anglia, together with the remaining service to Immingham Dock from Ulceby in Lincolnshire. Balanced against this rather depressing list of closures, we were pleased to welcome the Dart Valley Railway, which was reopened by preservationists with steam traction in April.

There was determination by the Government to reduce the number of days lost to strikes in British industry. A white paper entitled 'In Place of Strife' was introduced in January; in fact, the proposals gave rise to a great deal of strife between the Government and the TUC, and the ensuing legislation was rather different from what had originally been outlined.

More significant strife was taking place in Northern Ireland. Rioting in Derry in January left more than 100 people injured; in July and early August there had been further rioting in Derry and in Belfast. Matters were brought to a head when the Apprentice Boys March in Derry on 12 August led to a violent three-day riot that was soon called the 'Battle of the Bogside'. This led to the deployment of British troops in Ulster from 14 August.

For escapism, the cinema offered such delights as *Butch Cassidy and the Sundance Kid*, *The Italian Job* and *Midnight Cowboy*, while on television October saw the first programme of what in due course was to become a comedy

sensation – *Monty Python's Flying Circus*. Earlier in the year, television had given us the first ever glimpse of life behind the scenes in the Royal Family. On radio, the continued popularity of theatre and cinema organ music was recognised in a new series *The Organist Entertains*, which is still very popular on Radio 2 at the time of writing. April saw the end of *Mrs Dale's Diary*, which had survived the transition from the Light Programme to Radio 2 at the expense of being renamed *The Dales*; it was replaced by another serial, *Waggoners Walk*, which was to run until 1980.

Let us look back at a year when an average house in Britain cost £4,640, petrol cost 6s 2d (31p) per gallon and inflation was running at 5.6% – let's remember 1969…

Chris Harris, Poole, Dorset
November 2011

Background: **FARNHAM** The derelict points leading to the old ballast siding at the rear of Farnham shed were photographed on 3 January. Sadly further closures were to condemn a significant mileage of railway to similar dereliction during 1969.

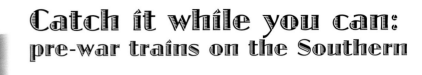

Catch it while you can: pre-war trains on the Southern

ALDERSHOT Although 1969 was the first full year without any scheduled steam workings on the British Rail network, there were still some delightful elderly carriages to ride in if you knew where to look for them. Parts of the Southern Region's electrified network were still operated by pre-war stock, as demonstrated by 2 BIL unit No 2005 at Aldershot on Wednesday 8 January; Guard Fred Jelley chats to a member of the station staff prior to giving the 'right away'.

ALDERSHOT On Friday 21 March sister 2 BIL unit No 2001 brings up the rear of a service to Alton, photographed at Aldershot. Both Nos 2001 and 2005 were part of the first batch of ten pre-production 2 BIL units, which came into service early in 1935; both were withdrawn later in 1969.

Below: **ASH** 2 BIL unit No 2138, seen at Ash on Sunday 25 May, was built in 1938 for the electrification of the lines between Waterloo and Reading. Notice that, in contrast to Nos 2001 and 2005, this unit has not been modified with two-tone warning horns, but retains its whistle, mounted above the wiper spigot beside the driver's windscreen. This unit's days were numbered, however; it was also withdrawn later in 1969.

Right: **ALDERSHOT** This view, taken through the van door of a Guildford to Ascot service on Tuesday 7 January, illustrates the outer end of the driving trailer composite coach of unit No 2058, which was awaiting its next turn of duty in the sidings at Aldershot. This was one of the batch of

2 BIL units delivered in 1937 for the Portsmouth and Alton electrification scheme and remained in service until 1971. The 2 BIL units were very comfortable to ride in, with well-cushioned seats and side corridors in both carriages, giving access to lavatories. Interior panelling was in teak or mahogany, and the overall ambience was well on a par with the Southern Railway's locomotive-hauled stock of the period. Introduced between 1935 and 1938, the 2 BIL units were quite long-lived, but their time was running out; 1969 saw the start of general withdrawals, many were dispensed with during 1970, and all had been taken out of service by the autumn of 1971.

within that coach to a lavatory. In contrast to the homely wood panelling of the 2 BIL units, the interior surfaces of the 2 HALs had stark Rexine finishes. Entering service on the line to Gillingham (Kent) in 1939 and transferring to the Western Section of the SR in 1958, No 2612 remained in service until 1970.

Below: **STAINES** On Friday 6 June 2 HAL unit No 2607 leads an eight-car formation into Staines forming the 1628 service from Waterloo; in this view the driving trailer composite is leading the train. No 2607 was also in service from 1939 until 1970.

Above: **CAMBERLEY** While the SR 2 BIL units were very comfortable and pleasant to travel in, the 2 HAL units that followed them were among the most austere electric multiple units (EMUs) ever to see service in the UK. Unit No 2612 is seen at Camberley after arrival with the 1458 service from Waterloo on 6 April. The compartments in the motor carriage, closest to the camera in this view, seated five across each side on uncomfortable bench seats; the driving trailer was only slightly better, with compartments seating four a side (three in 1st Class) with corridor access

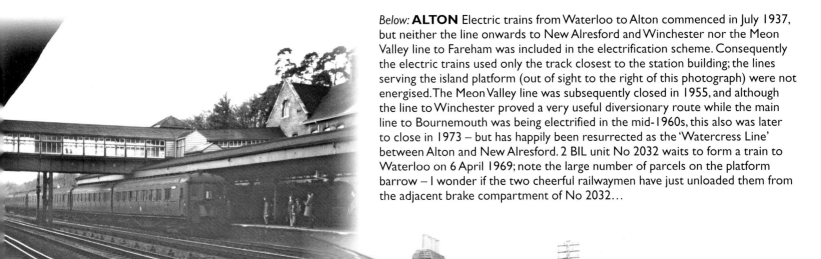

Below: **ALTON** Electric trains from Waterloo to Alton commenced in July 1937, but neither the line onwards to New Alresford and Winchester nor the Meon Valley line to Fareham was included in the electrification scheme. Consequently the electric trains used only the track closest to the station building; the lines serving the island platform (out of sight to the right of this photograph) were not energised. The Meon Valley line was subsequently closed in 1955, and although the line to Winchester proved a very useful diversionary route while the main line to Bournemouth was being electrified in the mid-1960s, this also was later to close in 1973 – but has happily been resurrected as the 'Watercress Line' between Alton and New Alresford. 2 BIL unit No 2032 waits to form a train to Waterloo on 6 April 1969; note the large number of parcels on the platform barrow – I wonder if the two cheerful railwaymen have just unloaded them from the adjacent brake compartment of No 2032…

Above: **WEYBRIDGE** Wednesday 2 January 1969 was a very dull day when Ray Ruffell photographed this six-car BIL/HAL/BIL formation entering Weybridge forming a stopping service from Portsmouth to Waterloo. By the summer of 1969 2 BIL and 2 HAL units were being ousted from the Portsmouth main line slow trains by new 4 VEP units; they largely disappeared from services between Waterloo and Reading the following year, with their final stamping ground being the lines along the South Coast between Portsmouth, Brighton, Eastbourne and Ore, where some examples remained in service until the summer of 1971.

PORTSMOUTH & SOUTHSEA The station here is effectively in two parts: the imposing entrance building leads to the low-level terminus platforms, which are seen in the picture below on Thursday 3 April with 2 HAL unit No 2654 at the head of a rake of HAL and BIL stock forming the 1600 stopping train to Waterloo. New in 1939, No 2654 was withdrawn from service in 1970. Out of sight to the left of this photograph is the high-level station, an island platform use by trains travelling to and from Portsmouth Harbour. The direct line from Waterloo to Portsmouth via Liphook was electrified in 1937; electric service from Victoria to Portsmouth via Horsham commenced the following year.

Sets of four-car EMUs were provided for the Portsmouth fast trains, and were designed to provide a corridor throughout the train rather than just within the individual units. These units were officially designated 4 COR, but their association with the Portsmouth route, together with their somewhat 'one-eyed' look as the result of the headcode panel being located in place of one of the cab windows, soon led to this stock becoming known as 'Nelsons'. In the second picture 4 COR unit No 3153, new in 1937 and remaining in service until 1972, is seen at the high-level platform leading the 1450 Waterloo to Portsmouth Harbour service on Friday 11 July 1969.

Below: **FRATTON** When the line from London to Brighton was electrified in 1933, three five-car all-Pullman EMUs (5 BEL) were provided for the 'Brighton Belle' service. These remained in service after the other stock provided for the Brighton electrification was replaced by more modern units in the mid-1960s. For most of their lives these unique units wore the traditional Pullman umber and cream livery, but in 1968/69 all three were overhauled at Eastleigh and repainted in blue and grey. When Ray Ruffell photographed unit No 3053 at Fratton on Tuesday 1 April 1969 it was making its last run in the traditional colours as it was on its way as empty stock to Eastleigh for overhaul and repaint. The 'Brighton Belle' ceased to run in April 1972, and the 5 BEL units were withdrawn. Fortunately all but one of the 15 carriages are still in existence, and at the time of writing a preservation scheme is aiming to restore and re-form a 5 BEL unit, which will be able to run under its own power on the electrified lines – an exciting project, which I hope will be successful.

Above: **FARNHAM** The carriage shed at Farnham, 820 feet long, with five roads, was built when the branch to Alton was electrified in 1937. In this photograph, taken in the shed on Thursday 2 January 1969, 4 COR No 3136 is seen on the left; new in 1937, this unit remained in service until 30 September 1972. On the right is 4 SUB unit No 4682, which was in service on the Southern Region from July 1950 until April 1983. The cheerful shunter, Cyril, stands beside the 4 SUB.

In search of steam

The second view shows Great Western Railway 'Hall' Class 4-6-0 No 4492 *Maindy Hall* which arrived at Barry in June 1964. In April 1974 this locomotive was purchased by the Great Western Society and moved to Didcot with the intention of rebuilding it as a 'Saint' Class 4-6-0 – the design from which the 'Hall' Class was developed. At the time of writing, work is proceeding on this project. *Both Brian Jackson*

BARRY By 1969 Woodham's scrapyard at Barry, South Glamorgan, had become the graveyard of many locomotives, although fortunately, owing to delays in breaking for scrap, a number were eventually saved for preservation. In the picture above, one of the former Somerset & Dorset 7F 2-8-0s, No 53809, stands among the carnage; almost symbolically, a tablet catcher protrudes from the footplate. Having arrived at Barry in August 1964, No 53809 was rescued in December 1975 for restoration, which was completed at the Midland Railway Centre at Butterley, and this locomotive has since worked enthusiasts' specials over the national rail network. Sister locomotive No 53808, which had arrived at Barry at the same time, is now preserved by the Somerset & Dorset Railway Trust on the West Somerset Railway.

Right: **BARRY** Great Western Railway 'Hall' Class 4-6-0 No 5900 *Hinderton Hall* had been dispatched to Barry in June 1964, and seven years later, in June 1971, was moved to Didcot following purchase by the Great Western Society. Following an extensive rebuild, *Hinderton Hall* was restored to main-line condition and for a period worked specials over the national rail network – something few people would have thought possible when this photograph was taken in 1969. *Brian Jackson*

Left: **TOTNES** The early beginnings of the Great Western Society were established on the Totnes Quay branch, where several items of GWR rolling stock together with 0-4-2 tank locomotive No 1466 and 0-6-0 saddle-tank No 1363 were assembled in 1964. The expansion of the Great Western Society saw its collection move away from Totnes, No 1363 being the last to depart on 1 May 1969; it is seen here days before the move took place. At the time of writing, No 1363 forms part of the Society's collection at Didcot, which is very well worth a visit. *Brian Jackson*

TWICKENHAM Locomotive No 4472 *Flying Scotsman* was built at
Doncaster Works in 1923 for the London & North Eastern Railway, and
after withdrawal by British Railways in 1963 was bought for preservation
by Alan Pegler. A notable event in 1968 had been the operation of a
special non-stop train from London to Edinburgh, and the following year
No 4472 and a special rake of stock was exported for a promotional
tour of the USA. Prior to departure on this overseas venture, No 4472
has attracted a number of admirers at Twickenham on Wednesday 20
August 1969 *(right)*. This station at Twickenham opened in March 1954,
situated to the east of the previous one; work on the new structure
had commenced in 1938 but was suspended after the outbreak of the
Second World War and not resumed until 1953.

The stock taken to the USA included one of the two Pullman
observation cars that had formerly run in the Devon Belle between

1947 and 1954. Car 14 *(left)*, seen at the end
of the train at Twickenham on the same day,
originated as an ambulance coach for the
London & North Western Railway in 1918;
it was converted into a Pullman Car in 1921
and rebuilt as an observation car at Pullman's
Preston Park, Brighton, workshops in 1947.
Financially the USA tour was not a success, but
fortunately No 4472 was repatriated in the
1970s, eventually being bought by the National
Railway Museum; at the time of writing it is
undergoing an extensive overhaul to main-line
running standard. Observation car 14 remained
in the USA until 2007, when it was returned
by sea to Southampton Docks, and at the time
of writing this historic coach resides at the
Swanage Railway in Dorset.

READING Huntley & Palmers was one of the best-known manufacturers of biscuits in the UK, and established a huge factory in Reading from 1846. The factory had its own internal railway system, which also linked it to the Great Western Railway sidings at Reading, together with a link to the Southern goods yard. Because the trains also had to work within the warehouses, conventional steam locomotives were not suitable owing to fumes and the danger of fire from sparks. Special fireless steam locomotives were used; these were filled up with high-pressure steam from a stationary boiler – a fill-up took 15 minutes and gave around 2 hours' running time. Huntley & Palmers' locomotive No 1 was built by W. G. Bagnall at Stafford in 1932, and was photographed during the evening of Wednesday 25 June 1969, the final year that the factory railway system was operational; biscuit manufacture in Reading ceased entirely in 1976.

NEASDEN Between 1956 and 1963 London Transport bought 11 pannier tank engines that were originally built in 1929/30 for the Great Western Railway. They were used on permanent way trains rather than passenger services, and three of them remained active on these duties until June 1971. They are glimpsed from a passing train at London Transport's Neasden depot on Sunday 24 August 1969.

Freight in focus

WOKING Just after sunrise on Wednesday 30 July, Class 47 diesel-electric locomotive No D1896 passes through Woking on the Stratford to Millbrook Freightliner service; the Millbrook Freightliner terminal, with three tracks, had opened the previous year. D1896 was built by Brush at its Falcon Works, and entered traffic on 7 September 1965. Allocated to Stratford depot at the time of this photograph, the locomotive was subsequently renumbered 47377 in 1974 and was withdrawn in May 2000.

By 1969 most of the platform signage at Woking had been updated using the then corporate black script on a white background, but the large green enamel signs on the ends of the platform canopies remain; notice also the traditional SR lamp standards visible above the Freightliner containers.

WIMBLEDON Class 47 diesel-electric No D1662 *Isambard Kingdom Brunel* was photographed at Wimbledon on Friday 8 August, heading a train of empty coal wagons that will return to South Wales via Salisbury, Westbury and the Severn Tunnel. Named after the famous first chief engineer of the Great Western Railway, who in 2002 was placed second behind Winston Churchill in a BBC TV poll to name the 100 'Greatest Britons', D1662 was built at British Railways' Crewe Works and entered traffic on 27 February 1965. It was renumbered 47484 in December 1973, and in 1985 was one of several locomotives to be repainted in Brunswick Green to mark the 150th Anniversary of the Great Western Railway. It was withdrawn from service in June 1998.

CLAPHAM JUNCTION This rake of empty wagons is being hauled through the Windsor line platforms at Clapham Junction by Class 46 'Peak' locomotive No D147. Built by British Railways Derby Works in December 1961, D147 was subsequently renumbered 46010 and was preserved following withdrawal by British Rail in November 1984. The girder structure visible above the roof of the signal box in the left background is a reminder of the Second World War, when it was erected to carry a second roof of steel sheeting over the box as an air raid precaution. This protective sheeting was removed after the bridge carrying the signal box partially failed during the height of the morning peak period on Monday 10 May 1965, resulting in the closure of Waterloo for the rest of that day to allow emergency repairs to be carried out.

Below: **WEYBRIDGE** Rail Express Parcels was an important part of the business in 1969. Hurrying towards London on the fast line through Weybridge station on 2 January, this working is headed by Class 73 electro-diesel locomotive No E6020. This was one of 49 versatile locomotives that could run as ordinary electrics from the live rail or, when the third rail supply was not available (for example, in shunting yards), could run, albeit at a reduced horsepower, from the on-board diesel generator. E6020 was built by English Electric at the Vulcan Foundry, Newton-le-Willows, in 1966 and worked to the Southern Region under its own diesel power. Renumbered 73114 under the TOPS scheme, this locomotive was named *Stewarts Lane Traction Maintenance Depot* in 1994 and was subsequently withdrawn from service in January 1999. Preserved after withdrawal, 73114 is at the Battlefield Railway in Leicestershire at the time of writing, and regularly hauls passenger trains using its diesel power.

Above: **WOKING** Two A1A-A1A Class 31 Brush Type 2 diesel locomotives are seen in charge of a train of cement wagons on Tuesday 15 April. British Railways took delivery of 263 locomotives of this type, and for a number of years they were particularly associated with the Eastern Region, but in due course they were seen throughout the railway network. When built they were equipped with Mirrlees engines, but these were replaced by English Electric Type 12SV units of 1,470bhp from 1964 onwards. Note that the front locomotive has the old-type route identity discs rather than a headcode panel. On the right is the driving trailer composite of a brand-new 4VEP unit, a type that was being brought into service in quantity at the time to replace pre-war Southern Railway EMUs.

A warm welcome to the Dart Valley Railway

Right: **BUCKFASTLEIGH** In April 1969 railway enthusiasts were delighted by the reopening of the Dart Valley Railway as a steam-operated heritage line. On a wet day, shortly before the reopening, two of the restored line's locomotives were photographed at Buckfastleigh. 2-6-2 tank No 4555 was the first locomotive to arrive at the preservation site, and was acquired immediately after withdrawal from BR service in 1965. Built by the Great

Western Railway at Swindon in 1924, this locomotive had hauled the last British Railways freight train on the branch in September 1962, and as such was an especially appropriate acquisition. At the time of writing, No 4555 is located on the Torbay Steam Railway. *Brian Jackson*

Left: **STAVERTON BRIDGE** Passengers alight from a Dart Valley Railway train at Staverton Bridge a few days after the line was reopened in April 1969. *Brian Jackson*

DART VALLEY The picturesque nature of the line is nicely illustrated as No 6412 propels its train beside the banks of the River Dart towards Staverton Bridge. The line had originally opened on 1 May 1872 as a branch from Totnes to Ashburton, and was worked by the South Devon Railway Company until 1876, when it was absorbed into the Great Western Railway. Always something of a quiet backwater, the line was closed to passengers in November 1958 and to freight in September 1962. North of Buckfastleigh, the trackbed on towards Ashburton was lost in 1971 as part of a scheme to widen the A38 road. However, in more recent years the railway has opened its own Riverside station at the other end of the line in Totnes, and this now provides a connection that is within easy walking distance of national rail services. *Brian Jackson*

BUCKFASTLEIGH Former Great Western Railway pannier tank No 6412 is sandwiched between four auto-coaches, waiting to depart from Buckfastleigh station in April 1969, several days after the line was reopened. Such was the enthusiasm that the 'Inaugural Special' headboard remained in place for a few weeks. *Brian Jackson*

F.W. Hawksworth, who was the last Chief Mechanical Engineer of the Great Western Railway, the auto-coach, seen in close-up in the second photograph, was built by British Railways at Swindon Works in 1951. The cab contains a regulator, connected by a system of rods and joints to the locomotive regulator, and a vacuum brake handle, enabling the driver to control the train from the front carriage while the fireman stays on the footplate. Note the large warning gong in place of a whistle. Operation of this beautiful heritage line passed to the South Devon Railway Trust in 1991; in the 21st century the line therefore operates under its original 1872 title as the South Devon Railway, and is well worth a visit. *Both Brian Jackson*

DART VALLEY Although Dart Valley Railway services commenced from Saturday 5 April 1969, the official reopening ceremony took place a few weeks later on Wednesday 21 May. The honours were carried out by Dr Richard Beeching, who commented, 'If I had not closed this branch, I could not now be reopening it.' However, as the branch had closed to passengers in 1958 and Dr Beeching was not appointed Chairman of the British Transport Commission until 1961,

the closure to passengers had actually been the responsibility of the Branch Line Committee within British Railways. The delightful Devon scenery forms a backdrop to No 6412 and its train in April 1969; seeing the locomotive in the centre of an auto-train was at one time a common sight on GWR lines. No 6412 was built at Swindon in 1934 for auto-train working, and had the honour of powering the first train on the reopened Dart Valley Railway.

Although built to a design by

1969 ARRIVALS & DEPARTURES

Births

Michael Schumacher	Racing driver	3 January
Stephen Hendry	Snooker player	13 January
Alexander McQueen	Fashion designer (d2010)	17 March
Cerys Matthews	Musician	11 April
Dion Dublin	Footballer	22 April
Cate Blanchett	Actress	14 May
Steffi Graf	Tennis player	14 June
Ashley Jensen	Actress	10 August
Justin Broadrick	Musician	15 August
Christian Slater	Actor	18 August
Joe Swail	Snooker player	29 August
Catherine Zeta Jones	Actress	25 September
Paul Warhurst	Football player	26 September
Gerard Butler	Actor	13 November
Richard Hammond	TV presenter	19 December
Ed Miliband	Politician	24 December

Deaths

Richmal Crompton	Writer (b1890)	11 January
Boris Karloff	Actor (b1887)	2 February
Kenneth Horne	Comedian (b1907)	14 February
John Wyndham	Writer (b1903)	11 March
Billy Cotton	Entertainer (b1899)	25 March
Alan Mowbray	Actor (b1896)	25 March
Dwight D. Eisenhower	34th US President (b1890)	28 March
Osbert Sitwell	Writer (b1892)	4 May
Rhys Williams	Actor (b1897)	28 May
Martita Hunt	Actress (b1900)	13 June
Judy Garland	Actress (b1922)	22 June
Brian Jones	Musician (b1942)	3 July
Leonard Woolf	Writer (b1890)	14 August
Dudley D. Watkins	Illustrator (b1907)	20 August
Ivy Compton-Burnett	Writer (b1884)	27 August
Jack Kerouac	Writer (b1922)	21 October
Ted Heath	Bandleader (b1902)	18 November
Princess Alice of Battenberg	(b1885)	5 December
Eric Portman	Actor (b1901)	7 December

LONGMOOR MILITARY RAILWAY: Army diesel-hydraulic 0-4-0 No 412, built by the North British Railway Co in 1959 (Works No 27647), is seen on 31 October 1969. This was the last day of operation at this once extensive system and can therefore be considered a 'departure' from the railway scene. Running between Liss and Bordon, with several junctions and spurs, construction of the railway began in 1903 as a narrow-gauge line to transport building materials from Longmoor camp to Bordon. Converted to standard gauge by 1908, the line developed as a training centre for the Army. The railway is now long gone, but traces of the trackbed can still be found today.

By diesel traction

Below: **WATERLOO** A race meeting at Salisbury on Saturday 19 July required the operation of a special train from London, and Class 205 'Hampshire' unit No 1105 is seen forming this working waiting to leave platform 15 at 1040. No 1105 was built at Eastleigh in 1957 as a two-car set for use on services between Portsmouth and Salisbury; the new diesel units were so successful on this route that more accommodation was needed, so centre trailer coaches were added in 1959. The race special is taking No 1105 slightly away from its usual stamping ground. After arrival at Salisbury station the punters will be taken by Wilts & Dorset buses onwards to Salisbury Race Course on the chalk downs near Netherhampton.

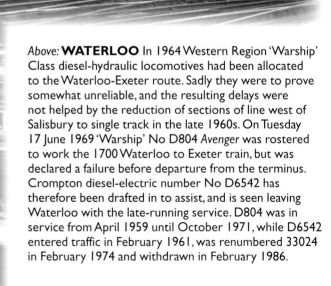

Above: **WATERLOO** In 1964 Western Region 'Warship' Class diesel-hydraulic locomotives had been allocated to the Waterloo-Exeter route. Sadly they were to prove somewhat unreliable, and the resulting delays were not helped by the reduction of sections of line west of Salisbury to single track in the late 1960s. On Tuesday 17 June 1969 'Warship' No D804 *Avenger* was rostered to work the 1700 Waterloo to Exeter train, but was declared a failure before departure from the terminus. Crompton diesel-electric number No D6542 has therefore been drafted in to assist, and is seen leaving Waterloo with the late-running service. D804 was in service from April 1959 until October 1971, while D6542 entered traffic in February 1961, was renumbered 33024 in February 1974 and withdrawn in February 1986.

SALISBURY Diversions as a result of engineering work are often a feature of rail travel on Sundays. On 6 July 1969 trains between Paddington and the West Country were being diverted from Reading via Basingstoke and Salisbury. On this very wet summer day Class 47 No D1607 is seen in the first picture pulling into Platform 2 at Salisbury station with the 1210 service from Paignton to Paddington, under the interested gaze of a number of lads at the platform end. D1607 was built at British Railways' Crewe Works in July 1964, was renumbered 47477 in March 1974 and withdrawn in September 1992.

A more unusual visitor to Salisbury that day, seen in the second view, was 'Western' Class 52 diesel-hydraulic No D1057 *Western Chieftain*, at the head of a westbound train of BR Standard Mark 1 stock in Platform 4. *Western Chieftain* was also built at Crewe Works; entering service on 6 April 1963, it was withdrawn in June 1977.

Below: **NORTH CAMP** The Class 33 diesels, built by the Birmingham Railway Carriage & Wagon Company and often referred to as 'Cromptons' on account of their Crompton Parkinson electric transmission, were the Southern Region's 'maids of all work' in 1969. Two members of the class are seen operating peak-period trains on the Reading to Redhill service on Tuesday 1 July. On the left is No D6548 with the 1705 from Reading to Redhill. Entering traffic in April 1961, this locomotive was later renumbered 33030 in January 1974 and withdrawn in December 1998, but reinstated a year later. It subsequently worked for EWS at Motherwell and for DRS, and at the time of writing is in the ownership of the West Coast Railway Company at Carnforth as a source of spares for other preserved examples of the same type. Approaching the camera, and displaying headcode 88, is No D6557 with the 1640 service from Redhill to Reading. D6557 entered traffic in June 1961, was renumbered 33039 in January 1974 and withdrawn in May 1989.

Above: **ALTON** A total of 19 'Cromptons' were modified so that they could work in multiple with 4TC trailer units in push-pull mode. This facility was mainly used between Bournemouth and Weymouth, but there were many instances when a 'Crompton' and a TC formation were used in other locations. A case in point is here at Alton on Friday 25 April, when No D6535 and TC unit 415 have deputised for the more usual Class 205 'Hampshire' unit on a service from Southampton. Mr Lowe, the Alton Station Master, stands beside the locomotive, which by all accounts had found propelling the four-coach train over the steep gradients from New Alresford quite taxing. At the further platform 2 HAL unit No 2627 provides the onward connection to Waterloo. No D6535 entered traffic in December 1960 and was modified for push-pull operation at Eastleigh in March 1967; the additional 'plumbing' on the front end will be readily noticed when compared with D6557 in the view on the left. Renumbered 33116 in May 1974, this locomotive was preserved after withdrawal in August 1998 and at the time of writing resides on the Great Central Railway at Loughborough, Leicestershire.

Below: **GUILDFORD** Owing to restricted clearances in several tunnels between Tunbridge Wells and Hastings, a special build of straight-sided diesel-electric multiple units was required when the service between Charing Cross and Hastings was modernised in the late 1950s. Included in the initial build were seven units that included a buffet coach in their six-car formations, entering traffic in 1958. On Saturday 16 August 1969 unit No 1036 has been appropriated for the Reading-Redhill-Tonbridge service, and is seen at Guildford with the 1724 service from Reading to Tonbridge; I wonder if the buffet car was staffed and open…

Above: **PORTSMOUTH & SOUTHSEA** Judging by the pristine state of the paintwork, it is likely that 'Tadpole' unit No 1204 has just received attention at Eastleigh Works; that could account for it being in one of the low-level platforms at Portsmouth & Southsea forming the 1608 service to Salisbury on Tuesday 15 April. This was one of six diesel-electric units made up in 1964 from two coaches of narrow-bodied Hastings-line stock together with a normal-size former 2 EPB driving trailer specifically to operate the Reading-Redhill-Tonbridge line. The difference in width between the leading two carriages and the full-width vehicle at the rear can be readily seen, illustrating how these units came by their nickname of 'Tadpoles'. The young, anorak-clad enthusiast on the platform seems unimpressed by this unusual visitor. 2 HAP EMU No 6035 stands on the adjacent line.

SANDHURST Special trains for service people were often chartered from British Railways. On Sunday 20 July 'Warship' diesel-hydraulic No D831 *Monarch* has charge of a troop special from North Camp to Plymouth. *Monarch* was new in January 1961 and was in traffic for just over ten years, being withdrawn in October 1971. When this photograph was taken, the locomotive was based at Laira, Plymouth.

Inset: **GUILDFORD** The Royal Navy personnel in this train are travelling almost the length of the UK – from Elgin to Portsmouth Harbour. Class 47 No D1707 hauls the special at Guildford; this locomotive entered traffic in January 1964, was renumbered 47487 in March 1974, and was withdrawn in December 1988. Notice that the water column still survives on Platform 4, a relic of the age of steam.

Catch it while you can: The silent service

Below: **CHRISTCHURCH** April 1969 saw the demise of the well-known Bournemouth Corporation trolleybus system. Trolleybus operation in Bournemouth had commenced in 1933, and the route to Christchurch opened in 1936. The undertaking's Bournemouth to Christchurch routes were the last to remain trolleybus-operated, and this ensured the survival of the unusual trolleybus turntable at the terminus off Church Street in Christchurch, which was first used on 19 June 1936. The only other trolleybus turntable in the UK was at Longwood on the Huddersfield system in West Yorkshire, where the equipment was only used as such for a few months from September 1939, so this example at Christchurch could be regarded as unique. The turntable was manually operated, and here the crew are heaving round Sunbeam MF2B No 273 (WRU 273) shortly before the system's closure. WRU 273 entered service on 1 January 1959 and was withdrawn after taking part in the final trolleybus procession on Sunday 20 April. *Brian Jackson*

Below right: **BOURNEMOUTH** The last day of trolleybus operation on normal scheduled services was Saturday 19 April. The following afternoon, a procession of trolleybuses, lettered A-S, ran from Bournemouth Pier via Boscombe, Southbourne, Christchurch and Iford to the depot at Mallard Road; vehicle letter S departed first, with A bringing up the rear. Number 282 (YLJ 282), letter R, waits at Pier Approach to pick up its allocated passengers as other trolleys in the procession queue up Bath Road. YLJ 282 had entered service in September 1959, and thus saw less than ten years of use. Appropriately, the final vehicle in the procession was 301 LJ, which in November 1962 was the final trolleybus to have been brought into scheduled service in the UK, and which was used as such for less than seven years. The

scene at this location has changed beyond all recognition in the 21st century; the Pier Approach Baths, seen on the right, have been demolished and replaced by a building intended for an Imax cinema (itself closed), while the Pavilion garage and Bath Road offices of Hants & Dorset Motor Services, seen on the left, have long gone. Road layout changes have seen the construction of a flyover in the foreground. *Brian Jackson*

BOURNEMOUTH Several preserved trolleybuses took part in the final procession on Sunday 20 April. Waiting in Bath Road we see ALJ 973, a Sunbeam MS2 that had been in service with Bournemouth Corporation from 1935 until 1963. Behind it is KLJ 346, a BUT vehicle that had been in the fleet from 1950 until 1966. Notice that these are both three-axle vehicles; they were lettered J and H respectively in the procession. *Brian Jackson*

1969 TV favourites

Civilisation: This 13-part BBC series, written and presented by Kenneth Clark, followed the story of civilisation from the fall of Rome through to the 1960s. Informative and entertaining, it was television at its best.

Paul Temple: The detective, created by Francis Durbridge, whose adventures we had previously enjoyed on the wireless (heralded by *Coronation Scot* as a signature tune), made the transition to television with an exciting colour series. *Take Three Girls:* Angela Down, Lisa Goddard and Susan Jameson starred in this popular series about three young ladies who shared a London flat.

Royal Family: A unique co-production by BBC and ITV, this documentary showed the private life of the Queen and the Royal Family for the first time on television.

Stars on Sunday: Presented by Jess Yates and featuring guests from show business and public life, this programme of hymns and Bible readings was later to become the first religious broadcast to enter the Top 20 most popular television shows.

Monty Python's Flying Circus: October 1969 saw the broadcast of the first programme of what must certainly be one of the greatest television comedies of all time. The Python team (John Cleese, Graham Chapman, Michael Palin, Terry Jones, Eric Idle and Terry Gilliam) put together some brilliant sketches for the innovative and hilarious series; one of their catchphrases was 'And now for something completely different' – this programme certainly was, and viewers loved it.

100 years of the District

WIMBLEDON On Sunday 24 August London Transport operated a special rail tour around the sub-surface part of its network to mark the centenary of the District Line, the first section of which – between South Kensington and Westminster – had opened 100 years previously. The special train was formed of Q stock, which was the oldest on the line at that time and consisted of batches of cars built between 1923 and 1938. The motor car at the 'West' end of the unit, photographed at Wimbledon, was built in 1923 by the Gloucester Carriage & Wagon Company. This distinctive batch of cars had a very angular and box-like appearance, which was accentuated by the clerestory being carried to the end of the bodywork and not rounded off. A train of District Line R stock is seen on the left forming a service train to Tower Hill.

The interior of 1923 Q stock motor car No 4204 is seen in the second photograph, taken during the tour. This car remained in service with London Transport until 1971, when all of the remaining Q stock was withdrawn.

Right: **WIMBLEDON** The Q stock motor car at the other end of the train was from the batch built by the Birmingham Railway Carriage & Wagon Company in 1927. This type of car was usually found at the 'East' end of District Line Q stock trains, as seen here, although a small number were turned to operate at the 'West' end after the introduction of the R stock led to a reorganisation of District Line cars.

Below: **UXBRIDGE** Designed by Charles Holden, this station at Uxbridge was opened in December 1938 on a new alignment, replacing an earlier terminal that was less conveniently situated. Admiring enthusiasts and staff have gathered round the venerable 1923 motor carriage on the special train. When comparing the front ends of the 1923 and 1927 cars illustrated on this page, note the external destination boards and widely spaced marker lights fitted with outside shades on the 1923 stock, which contrast with the destination display and neat panel of marker lights controlled from within the cab of the 1927 stock.

January
- Rupert Murdoch purchases the *News of the World*, at that time the UK's largest selling Sunday newspaper.
- Closure of the Waverley Route (Edinburgh-Carlisle via Hawick) to passengers.
- Protests by students close the London School of Economics, which does not reopen for three weeks.

February
- Yasser Arafat becomes leader of the Palestine Liberation Organisation.
- The Boeing 747 'Jumbo' jet makes its first test flight.

March
- Concorde's first test flight
- Official opening of the London Transport Victoria Line by Her Majesty the Queen.

April
- United Kingdom voting age is lowered from 21 to 18.
- Robin Knox-Johnston becomes the first person to sail non-stop around the world single-handed.

May
- Launch of the Austin Maxi, Britain's first production hatchback car.
- Maiden voyage of the liner *Queen Elizabeth 2* to New York.

June
- The United Kingdom and Rhodesia sever diplomatic links.

CHESHAM The tour reached Chesham, deep in the heart of 'Metroland', where the normal service was provided by Metropolitan Line Class A stock dating from 1960-62, as seen on the left. For many years London Transport had provided a steam-worked push-pull shuttle service between Chesham and Chalfont & Latimer; this arrangement continued until September 1960, when the branch was converted to electric working. Four of the carriages that had been used on this shuttle service, and which date back to 1898, are preserved on the Bluebell Railway in Sussex.

Catch it while you can:
the changing railway scene

Above: **GUILDFORD** As the 1960s drew to a close, the railway was changing quickly, and scenes that had remained unaltered for many years were being transformed as the new British Rail corporate image spread across the network. In particular remnants of steam traction were fast disappearing. The shed at Guildford, originally opened by the LSWR in 1887, had closed on the last day of Southern Region steam, 9 July 1967. Almost two years later, on Saturday 8 March 1969, Ray Ruffell photographed the erstwhile coal stage in the course of demolition.

Left: **ASCOT** Dating from 1889, the days of this timber-built single-road shed were numbered when this photograph was taken on Wednesday 25 June; it was demolished later in the year, in September.

Right: **DORCHESTER WEST** The line from Yeovil to Dorchester and Weymouth was opened in 1857. Originally built to the Great Western Railway broad gauge, the route was converted to standard gauge in 1874. In 1950 the route was transferred from the Western Region to the Southern Region of British Railways, but this was reversed 12 years later in 1962, except that Dorchester West station remained the responsibility of the Southern. By 1969 the goods shed had fallen into disuse, the goods yard having closed on 6 September 1965. The building dated back to the broad gauge era, but now stood isolated from the line. Happily the passenger station at Dorchester West remains open in 2011, served by First Great Western trains running between Bath and Weymouth. *Brian Jackson*

Below: **WESTHAM HALT** Work proceeds apace to demolish the level crossing at Westham Halt on the former Weymouth-Portland branch. Opened in October 1865, the branch had closed to passenger traffic in March 1952 and to freight in April 1965. *Brian Jackson*

The changing railway scene

MONKTON & CAME HALT Opened on 1 June 1905 to serve a nearby golf course as well as the two hamlets from which its name was derived, Monkton & Came Halt originally had wooden platforms and 'pagoda'-type shelters. After the Second World War the platforms were reconstructed as seen here, but the halt was closed on 7 December 1957. Apart from the removal of the waiting shelters, the former halt still looks in reasonable condition 12 years later. Since 1988 this line has been served by electric trains, and few people will now remember Monkton & Came Halt. *Brian Jackson*

BASINGSTOKE A sad sight on Thursday 19 June was this train made up of condemned electric stock that had been built for the 1933 Brighton line electrification. Notice that the carriage closest to the guard's van has severe straight sides compared with the other carriages in the train. This vehicle is of particular interest; it is a prototype that was built by the Birmingham Railway Carriage & Wagon Company in 1931 and was used in various trials before being formed into one of the 6 CIT sets. It ended its days as part of 6 COR unit No 3041, one of ten units made up in 1965-66 from withdrawn Brighton line stock that were used on relief and special workings for a few years until withdrawal.

Above: **UFTON CROSSING** This austere, box-like signal cabin beside the Berks & Hants line was opened on 14 February 1943 by the Great Western Railway. It replaced an earlier structure, as additional signalling was required to control the up and down goods running loops that had been installed between Ufton and Aldermaston to handle additional wartime traffic. The up goods loop had been taken out of use in March 1963, but the signal box, crossing gates and an attractive old lamp were still in use when photographed during the summer of 1969. The signal box was subsequently closed on 19 September 1977. Sadly, Ufton Crossing was in the news on 6 November 2004 when a High Speed Train hit a car on the crossing, a tragedy in which seven people lost their lives and 150 were injured. *Brian Jackson*

Above right: **WEYMOUTH** In 1969 British Rail still operated shipping services for both passengers and freight. During the Christmas layover of that year, five railway ships were in port at Weymouth, including the two cargo vessels seen here. MV *Winchester* was built by Denny of Dumbarton and launched in March 1947 as a cargo ship for the Channel Islands route, replacing tonnage lost during the Second World War. Sold in 1971, she saw further service in the waters around Greece until broken up in 1995. Astern of the *Winchester* lays MV *Moose*; built in 1959 as a replacement for older vessels on the Southampton-Channel Islands cargo route, in her later years she sailed from Weymouth until the freight service was withdrawn, after which she was disposed of to Greek interests, and eventually broken up in 1995. *Brian Jackson*

STOKE CANON The 1955 Modernisation Plan for British Railways led to the ordering and construction of large numbers of diesel locomotives. In general British Railways opted for diesel-electric locomotives, but the Western Region initially favoured the diesel-hydraulic type. The final batch of main-line diesel-hydraulic locomotives delivered to the Western Region entered service from the end of 1961, and were the 74 'Western' Class 52s. An unidentified member of the class comes out of the setting sun and passes Stoke Canon signal box with an up train on a summer evening in 1969. The 'Westerns' were withdrawn between 1973 and 1977, but several survive in preservation. *Brian Jackson*

DAWLISH WARREN Another unidentified 'Western' speeds past Dawlish Warren on the down fast line during the summer of 1969. Despite the diesel locomotive and the blue and grey livery of the BR Standard stock forming the train, plenty of period charm remained at that time; note in particular the station buildings on the up platform, still complete with their traditional enamel signage in Western Region brown. *Brian Jackson*

1969 No 1 Records

January

Ob-La-Di Ob-La-Da	Marmalade
Albatross	Fleetwood Mac

February

Blackberry Way	Move
(If Paradise Is) Half As Nice	Amen Corner
Where Do You Go To My Lovely	Peter Starstedt

March

I Heard It Through The Grapevine	Marvin Gaye

April

Israelites	Desmond Dekker & The Aces

May

Get Back	Beatles

June

Dizzy	Tommy Roe
The Ballad of John and Yoko	Beatles

July

Something in the Air	Thunderclap Newman
Honky Tonk Women	Rolling Stones

August

In the Year 2525	Zager & Evans

September

Bad Moon Rising Creedence Clearwater Revival	

October

Je T'Aime...Moi Non Plus	Jane Birkin & Serge Gainsbourg
I'll Never Fall In Love Again	Bobbie Gentry

November

Sugar Sugar	Archies

December

Two Little Boys	Rolf Harris

A little mishap...

WATERLOO On Friday 5 December 1969 at around 1415 the eight BR Standard Mark 1 carriages that had formed the 1015 service from Exeter St David's to Waterloo were drawn forward out of Platform 14 onto the down Windsor local line in order to release the locomotive that had brought the train from Exeter. This achieved, the carriages were intended to be propelled back into Platform 14. Unfortunately a signalman had inadvertently set a route into Platform 12, and although one ground signal had been cleared, neither the shunter in charge of the movement nor the driver had noticed that a second ground

signal remained at Danger because Platform 12 was already occupied. The propelled carriages, travelling between 5 and 10mph, struck the stock of the 1557 van train from Waterloo, which had been standing in Platform 12. A number of the vans were damaged and three came into contact with the REP/TC formation that was standing in the adjacent Platform 13, forming the 1430 service to Weymouth. Fortunately there were no serious injuries, as much of the damage to the Weymouth train was caused to the brake-van section of the leading 4TC unit. Two passenger and three parcels trains were cancelled as a result of the accident, but otherwise only slight delays were caused to the service, and everything had been made good by 0615 the following morning. These photographs were taken after the stock of the Weymouth and Exeter trains had been removed, and illustrate quite conclusively that 'two into one won't go'.

A sojourn in Wales

MACHYNLLETH Opened in 1863, Machynlleth station still retained some infrastructure from its original Cambrian Railways days when photographed in 1969, although the signal box on the left is a modern British Railways structure. The shed on the right was formerly home to a number of GWR 'Dukedog' Class 4-4-0 locomotives that were once a familiar sight on this line. By 1969, following the demise of steam, the shed played host to British Railways diesel multiple units (DMUs). At the time of writing, Machynlleth is served by Arriva Trains Wales, which in 2007 opened a new depot at this location for the Class 158 DMUs used on this route. *Brian Jackson*

PORTMADOC The Ffestiniog Railway was built between 1833 and 1836 to carry slate from Blaenau Ffestiniog to the coast at Portmadoc, where it was loaded into ships. Horse and gravity operation was used initially, but the introduction of steam locomotives in 1863 enabled a passenger service to be provided from 1865; this was the first narrow gauge railway in the UK to carry passengers. The line was closed to passengers in 1939 and to slate in 1946. Preservationists have since restored the passenger service in stages, starting with the section between Portmadoc and Boston Lodge in 1955 and finally reaching Blaenau Ffestiniog in 1982. *Blanche*, seen waiting for her next duty at Portmadoc in 1969, had been built in 1893 by the Hunslet Engine Company for the Penrhyn Quarry Railway and was acquired by the Ffestiniog Railway in 1963. *Brian Jackson*

PORTMADOC By 1969 the Ffestiniog Railway had been reopened to passengers from Portmadoc to Dduallt, a remote location with no road access that was to remain the northern terminus of the line until 1978. Double-ended Fairlie locomotive *Merddin Emrys*, named after a 6th-century Welsh poet, was built in the railway's own workshops at Boston Lodge in 1879 to the design of Percy Spooner. It worked the line until closure to slate traffic in 1946 and was returned to traffic in 1961 following restoration. *Brian Jackson*

1969 Happenings (2)

July
- Investiture of Charles, Prince of Wales.
- 'A small step for man, a giant leap for mankind': Neil Armstrong, leading the Apollo 11 mission, becomes the first man to walk on the Moon.

August
- The pre-decimal halfpenny ceases to be legal tender.
- Serious rioting in Northern Ireland leads to the deployment of British troops.
- Second Isle of Wight pop festival draws a crowd of 150,000.

September
- Colonel Gaddafi comes to power in Libya after a coup ousts King Idris.
- The Beatles release their *Abbey Road* album, their final LP recorded together.

October
- Introduction of the 50p piece as a replacement for the 10-shilling note in preparation for decimalisation of UK currency (which took place in February 1971).

November
- Regular colour television broadcasts begin on BBC1 and ITV.
- Apollo 12 moon landing.
- John Lennon returns his OBE in protest at the British Government's support for the US in the Vietnam War.

December
- Abolition of capital punishment is made permanent by the UK Parliament.
- Eleven people die in a fire at a Saffron Walden hotel on Boxing Day.

were designed and built in Switzerland. An unidentified example is seen shunting at Llanberis, while a train waiting to depart for the summit can be seen in the background. *Brian Jackson*

Below: **LLANBERIS** A Snowdon Mountain Railway train prepares to depart from the lower terminal at Llanberis during the summer of 1969. The locomotive is always kept at the lower end of the train, and is not coupled to the carriage that it is pushing to the summit; the train is protected by an automatic emergency braking system. The carriages were originally built open above the waist, with canvas side curtains for inclement weather; they were rebuilt to their current enclosed form between 1951 and 1957. Subject to weather conditions, trains run over the full 5-mile route between Llanberis and the summit from May until October; from March until May they normally run between Llanberis and Clogwyn only. *Brian Jackson*

Above: **LLANBERIS** The summit of the highest mountain in Wales, Mount Snowdon, is 3,570 feet above sea level. This peak can be reached by a number of paths, such as the Pyg Track or the Watkin Path, which vary in the degree of challenge they offer to walkers. The mountain was used by Edmund Hillary and his group in training for the ascent of Mount Everest in 1953. However, many people make the ascent the easy way by taking the Snowdon Mountain Railway train from Llanberis. Opened in 1896, this is Britain's only rack-and-pinion railway, with a maximum gradient of 1 in 5.5. The steam locomotives for the line

Down in the woodlands

BICTON PARK The beautiful Bicton Park Botanical Gardens are situated in the picturesque Otter Valley in East Devon. When the gardens were being prepared for public display in 1962, the estate staff built an 18-inch-gauge railway as an added attraction for visitors. Two steam locomotives, together with much of the rolling stock, came from Royal Arsenal Railway, Woolwich, and the railway opened to passengers in 1963. The railway is seen here running through its delightful woodland setting during the summer of 1969; sadly the nearby British Rail station at East Budleigh had closed just over two years earlier, in March 1967. It is still possible to enjoy a ride on the Bicton Railway in the 21st century; the gardens, and the railway – now the only 18-inch-gauge leisure line left in Britain – are open all year round. However, in 2000 the steam locomotives were replaced by a custom-built diesel-powered replica tank engine named *Sir Walter Raleigh*, the original stock having been sold to Waltham Abbey Royal Gunpowder Mills, where it is not operational at the time of writing, although the aim is to reconstruct an 18-inch-gauge railway to enable visitors to enjoy travelling round that site by steam. *Both Brian Jackson*

Catch it while you can: suburban variety

WINDSOR & ETON RIVERSIDE I hope I may be forgiven for including this Royal Borough as part of suburbia, but the rail journey is only 26.75 miles from Waterloo and the pattern of service provided is certainly suburban in nature. The London & South Western Railway branch to Windsor opened in 1849, although the imposing Riverside station, designed by Sir William Tite, was not completed until 1851. A feature of the station was a special waiting room built for Queen Victoria, located away from the public entrance and concourse; its turret and spirelet can be seen above the roof of the train in the centre of the photograph, taken on Tuesday 3 June. The area in the right foreground of this view is now a car park, while offices have been built where the train on the right stands at a platform outside of the main train shed. The semaphore signalling was replaced by colour lights during the 1970s. Happily Tite's handsome station building and spacious concourse remain and, although the booking office has been moved from its former grandiose accommodation, the station is still staffed.

Windsor Castle, seen in the background, is one of Her Majesty the Queen's three official residences, and is the largest occupied castle in the world.

Right: **CLAPHAM JUNCTION** The comfortable 2 BIL units were still often to be seen on the Waterloo to Alton services when this photograph was taken on Thursday 1 May. Unit No 2054 leads the 1553 departure from Waterloo on the approach to Clapham Junction; new in 1937, it was withdrawn in 1970. Notice the carriage wash visible in the background.

Below: **CLAPHAM JUNCTION** A good proportion of the Southern Region suburban services from Waterloo for many years were provided by the 4 SUB units. Designed by Oliver Bulleid with a view to providing as many seats as possible, early 4 SUB units were of compartment layout, seating six passengers across. This was a laudable aim, but it proved impossible to provide seats for all those who wished to travel at peak

periods, and standing among people's knees in a cramped compartment was a particularly uncomfortable way to travel. Later batches of 4 SUB units featured mostly saloon accommodation, although one compartment trailer carriage was included. A door to every compartment or seating bay ensured quick loading and unloading; and these rugged and reliable units gave sterling service to commuters for more than 30 years. Unit No 4719, heading for Waterloo from Clapham Junction with a service off the Hounslow loop on Wednesday 30 July, was built towards the end of the production of 4 SUB units, being completed in March 1951; it remained in service until June 1983.

Right: **HOUNSLOW** A feature of suburban operations is that provision has to be made for the large numbers of people who need to travel during the morning and evening peak periods on weekdays. Quite a number of the trains needed for this commuter traffic are not needed at other times, and although this does give opportunities for daytime maintenance and cleaning, it is unfortunate that this stock is not being used in revenue-earning service. The Hounslow loop in South West London was electrified in 1916, and this in turn led to increased residential development close to the line during the inter-war period. Extra sidings for electric stock were completed at Hounslow station in 1939, and are shown 30 years later during the daytime on Wednesday 20 August 1969 as 4 SUB units, together with a few 2 BILs in the distance, await their return to service for the evening peak. The semaphore signalling was replaced by colour lights in 1974.

Left: **WOKING** During severe winter weather, ice forming on the conductor rail is a hazard on lines with third-rail electrification. The reduced conductivity because of the ice leads to severe arcing, which can cause costly damage to trains. For many years, special de-icing trains were operated when necessary, spraying a special oil-based de-icing fluid onto the conductor rails. De-icing unit 003 had been newly converted in time for the 1969-70 winter when it was photographed at Woking on Friday 19 September. The two carriages forming this unit had entered service in 1940 in the two additional 4 LAV units (2954 and 2955) provided that year. Initially used mainly on the Waterloo-Bournemouth line, No 003 was later modified to spread a special compound on the running rails to improve adhesion during the autumn leaf fall season, and worked throughout the Southern Region. Withdrawn from service in 1989, No 003 was eventually scrapped in 1993.

STAINES Many commuters are creatures of habit who stand in the same place on the platform each morning to catch their train. Very often the front carriages of morning peak trains into London are the heaviest loaded so that people can make a quick dash for office or Underground on arrival. 2 HAL unit No 2682 leads a mixed HAL/BIL formation into Staines on a service from Camberley to Waterloo during the morning peak on Wednesday 9 April. Built in 1939, No 2682 was still equipped with a whistle rather than two-tone air horns when photographed; it was withdrawn from service in 1970. The intending passengers we see waiting in the sunshine will be travelling at the rear of the train, probably knowing from experience that it will be less crowded at that time of day. The tracks curving away to the right run to Windsor & Eton Riverside.

STAINES At the other end of the station on Monday 2 June, headcode 18 shows that the train approaching the camera is destined for Weybridge and Windsor; it will be divided during the stop at Staines. Unit No 5672 at the front of the train is one of a batch of 34 2 EPB units built in 1959, reusing the underframes from withdrawn 2 NOL units. Because of their 62-foot length, these carriages were therefore given Bulleid rather than BR Standard-style bodywork – a full 11 years after nationalisation. They were the very last Bulleid-style carriages to be built, and formed the mainstay of the Waterloo-Windsor/Weybridge route until 1974, when the majority were transferred to the Central Division of the Southern Region. Making its way towards London from the other platform, 2 HAL unit No 2627, in service from 1939 until 1971, brings up the rear of a train from Reading to Waterloo.

Below: **LITTLE SANDHURST** A reminder that time was running out for the pre-war EMUs as Class 33 diesel-electric No D6581 heads a train of condemned 2 BIL units on their way from storage sidings at Gatwick Airport to scrapping at Long Marston. The date is Saturday 8 November, and as 1969 drew to a close many of us realised that, quite apart from the recent demise of steam on the main-line network, we needed to make the most of the variety of stock that remained – since, as Bob Dylan had reminded us four years earlier, 'The times they are a-changing'. Yes, the new units that were coming into service in quantity were bright and modern inside, and many stations were considerably brightened up when they received the new corporate identity, but nonetheless a certain element of character was soon to be lost for ever.

Above: **CLAPHAM JUNCTION** This view, taken on Wednesday 30 April, shows a long rake of 4 COR units in the yard at Clapham Junction, awaiting their next call to duty on the Waterloo-Portsmouth line. These 1937 units held sway on the Portsmouth line fast trains until 1970/71, and many saw further use on Waterloo-Reading and on South Coast local services before the final examples were withdrawn in 1972.

In 1969 it was still possible to find lots of nostalgic treats to delight the observer while travelling, but the situation was changing as modernisation proceeded and British Rail corporate identity spread further across the network. Notice the new-style signs warning of the dangers of the live rail and proclaiming the identity of Clapham Junction C signal box.

BEAULIEU Our final look back at 1969 takes us to the Beaulieu Motor Museum, where former Southern Railway 4-4-0 'Schools' Class No 928 *Stowe* was on display together with three Pullman carriages dating from the 1920s. Lord Montagu had purchased *Stowe* after it was withdrawn by British Railways in 1962, together with the three superannuated Pullman carriages, and the ensemble was put on display at the museum in 1964. From that time the exhibit was entitled 'Bournemouth Belle', but until 9 July 1967 it was still possible to travel in Pullman carriages of similar vintage in the real train of that name – often hauled by steam, albeit a post-war Bulleid 'Pacific'. By 1969 that particular luxury train was just a fond memory, and this representation at Beaulieu evoked pleasantly nostalgic feelings for many people. The 'Bournemouth Belle' display remained at Beaulieu until 1973, when *Stowe*, which had been built at Eastleigh Works in 1934, was moved to Cranmore on the East Somerset Railway. Subsequently the locomotive moved again to the Bluebell Railway in 1980, and was restored to running order in 1981; at the time of writing this grand locomotive, which achieved the highest maximum recorded speed for a 'Schools' Class (95mph between Dorchester and Wareham in 1938), is out of service for overhaul. One of the three Pullman carriages from the Beaulieu display, *Fingall*, built by the Birmingham Carriage & Wagon Company in 1924, also passed in due course to the Bluebell Railway. *Brian Jackson*

Acknowledgements

It would not have been possible to produce this book without making use of two very extensive photograph collections. Many of the illustrations started in the camera of the late Ray Ruffell. Ray was a railwayman by profession, but his interest in transport went far beyond his day-to-day work. In his off-duty time, Ray travelled widely, and in so doing created an extensive photographic record of the railway system during a period when great change was under way.

Other photographs in this volume were taken by Brian Jackson, a fellow transport historian who has also travelled extensively across the UK armed with his camera to record the ever-changing transport scene. My warm thanks to Brian for allowing me to use some of the photographs he took during 1969.

Many scenes that were everyday and commonplace when Ray or Brian photographed them have now been swept away for ever, and the memories captured on film, precious at the time, are now beyond price. It is pleasing to record that the late Ray Ruffell's collection of photographs has been kept complete and is now in the safe keeping of The Nostalgia Collection, forming an important part of the company's photographic archives.

I would like to say a sincere thank you to the team at The Nostalgia Collection for inviting me to write this book. The cheerful and willing help I have received from Peter Townsend, Dave Walshaw and Will Adams has been very much appreciated, and I feel deeply honoured to work with such kind people.

I hope you have enjoyed this look back at 1969 and that you will wish to sample more years in the 'Railways & Recollections' series.

Index

GUILDFORD An example of how Ray Ruffell always had his camera at the ready to capture the railway scene. This 20-ton goods brake van was of a type built by the LMS at Derby Works between 1933 and 1947; M 731512 is seen visiting Southern Region metals on Wednesday 20 August.